Richard III (1452–85) reigned for only two years and two months, from June 1483 to August 1485, but the suspicion that he murdered his nephews, the 'Princes in the Tower', coupled with Shakespeare's brilliant character assassination has made him easily the most notorious – and controversial – of English monarchs. Time did not allow him to see all parts of his kingdom, but he was familiar with Leicester, which he visited on at least four occasions between 1483 and 1484. He stayed at the castle from 17–20 August 1483 in the course of his post-coronation 'progress', or tour of England, and was back on 22–23 October mustering troops to oppose the rebellion of his former ally, the Duke of Buckingham. On 31 July 1484 he spent a night

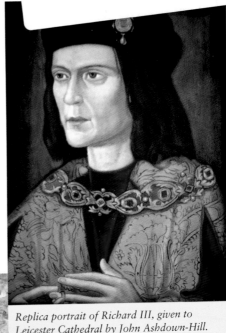

Replica portrait of Richard III, given to Leicester Cathedral by John Ashdown-Hill.

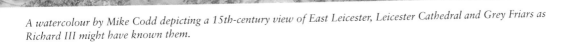

A watercolour by Mike Codd depicting a 15th-century view of East Leicester, Leicester Cathedral and Grey Friars as Richard III might have known them.

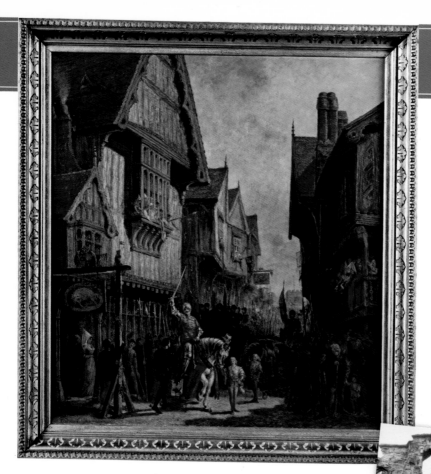

John Fulleylove's painting of 1880 illustrates the continuing impact of the King's story and connections with the city of Leicester.

The Turret Gateway at Leicester Castle.

at St Mary's Abbey, beyond the north wall, while travelling from Nottingham to Westminster, and broke a similar journey either there or in the town on 5 November. We know of these visits because Richard happened to issue an order or sign a document, but there could be others that passed unrecorded or unremarked.

Leicester had long been a stronghold of the vanquished House of Lancaster, and so the Yorkist Richard wanted to establish a good relationship with the townsfolk. The abbot of St Mary's was given permission to hold an annual fair in the abbey and in the parish of St Leonard for two days before the saint's feast day and for two afterwards; and when the dean and canons of the collegiate church in the Newarke complained that royal officials were witholding the revenues of some Welsh lands that formed part of their endowment, Richard authorised them to appoint a representative to visit the area, ascertain how much was owed, and enforce payment. Local men who had offended against the King's laws were pardoned, and on 24 November 1484 Richard – 'in consideration of the true and faithful service which our well-beloved Mayor and burgesses of our town of Leicester have rendered to us, as also in relief of their costs had and borne in this behalf, as also of the great ruin and decay in which the aforesaid town now is' – granted them an annuity of £20 for 20 years.

Local Myths and Legends

There are several stories about Richard's time in the city that have passed into local legend. Leicester's central location made it an ideal place to assemble forces to resist threats from all parts of the country, and Richard used it as a rallying point when Henry Tudor's invading army approached the Midlands in August 1485. He arrived on either Friday 19 or Saturday 20 August and, according to tradition, lodged at the White Boar Inn in High Street, the modern Highcross Street. The name of the inn was allegedly changed to the *Blue* Boar (a badge of the Lancastrian Earl of Oxford) in the aftermath of the battle of Bosworth, and the travelling bedstead Richard is said to have left there is now displayed at Donington-le-Heath Manor House, near Coalville in north-west Leicestershire. There is a story that a later landlady, a Mrs Clark,

The Blue Boar Inn, originally called the White Boar Inn.

Richard III's bed, on display at Donington-le-Heath Manor House. The house and gardens are open to the public.

found a large amount of money concealed in it and was murdered for her wealth in James I's reign. She was certainly killed and her attackers condemned and executed: but the King's bed was not mentioned at their trial and there is reason to believe that her riches owed more to hard work than to luck.

Richard marshalled his army in the town on the morning of Sunday 21 August and marched out over Bow Bridge, in the words of a contemporary, 'with great triumph and pomp'. Sir Richard Baker wrote in about 1625 that 'upon this bridge stood a stone of some height; against which King Richard, as he passed toward Bosworth, by chance struck his spur: and against the same stone, as he was brought back, hanging by the horse-side, his head was dashed and broken: as a

RICHARD III

Left: Locals enjoy a Richard III coronation pageant in Leicester in 1911.

Below: The myth that the body of the King was disinterred at the time of the Dissolution and thrown into the River Soar, under Bow Bridge, was mentioned by John Speed 'as tradition hath delivered' in 1611. The legend continued to grow until this plaque was erected on Bow Bridge in 1856. It now carries a disclaimer, erected by the Richard III Society.

wise woman (forsooth) had foretold: who before his going to battle, being asked of his success, said, that where his spur struck, his head should be broken.' Baker makes it clear that he was only reporting hearsay however, and so was John Nichols, the historian of Leicester, who noted another story included in a work entitled *Ten Strange Prophecies* published in 1644. According to this:

The original Bow Bridge was demolished in 1861 but its replacement was designed by the city as a memorial to Richard III, its ironwork depicting the white rose of York, the Tudor rose of Lancaster, Richard's white boar emblem and his motto 'Loyaulte me Lie' (Loyalty Binds Me).

'... as King Richard the Third, before the battle of Bosworth, rode through the south [sic] gate of Leicester; a poor old blind man (by profession a wheelwright) sat begging, and, hearing his approach, said, that if the Moon changed twice that day, having by her ordinary course changed in the morning, King Richard should lose his crown, and be slain. And a nobleman that carried the Moon for his colours revolted; thereby he lost his life and kingdom.'

The moon and the nobleman in question are not readily identifiable, but Lord Thomas Stanley's arms incorporated three plates argent (silver or white discs), which could be taken for full moons, while those of his brother Sir William were differenced by a crescent (moon) indicating that he was a second son. Their disloyalty undoubtedly contributed to Richard's downfall, but again, it may be a case of someone being wise after the event.

The Blue Boar Inn was demolished in 1836 and Bow Bridge rebuilt in 1861, but drawings exist showing how both might have appeared in Richard's day. Much of late medieval Leicester has disappeared with the passing of the centuries, but there are still a number of buildings the King would have recognised. He would surely have been impressed by the Norman Great Hall of the castle, 'the oldest surviving aisled and bay-divided hall in Europe', which he would have seen before it acquired its late 17th-century brick frontage and before panelling obscured the interior. He almost certainly worshipped in the castle church of St Mary 'de Castro', and would have at least noticed the four other surviving medieval churches: All Saints (which he would have passed as he rode into Leicester from Nottingham),

St Margaret's, St Martin's (now the cathedral) and St Nicholas. Some of their fabric has since been restored, but among the more notable surviving medieval features are the Norman sedilia in the chancel of St Mary 'de Castro'; the tower of St Nicholas, which incorporates courses of herringbone masonry formed by Roman tiles; the unusual projecting, perhaps once detached, tower of All Saints; and the rare 15th-century oak-vaulted roof with fan tracery in the north porch of St Martin's. Little remains of St Mary's Abbey, but the alabaster tomb of Richard's contemporary John Penny, who was abbot from 1496 to 1508, is preserved in St Margaret's church.

If Richard took the short walk from the castle through the Turret Gateway he would have entered the Newarke, the complex of buildings founded and extended by Henry Earl

The Great Hall at Leicester Castle.

St Mary 'de Castro' Church from Castle Yard.

Left: The 'Magazine' Gateway in the Newarke.

Below left: The interior of the 'Magazine' Gateway in the Newarke.

begun in 1536. If Henry VIII's plan to create 13 new dioceses had been brought to fruition it would have become the cathedral of a re-founded diocese of Leicester, but instead it lay in ruins by 1590. Richard could not have foreseen that his naked body would be displayed there in the aftermath of the Battle of Bosworth, a gesture designed to scotch rumours that he had somehow survived the conflict. Two restored arches in De Montfort University's Hawthorn Building are all that remain of the church today.

of Lancaster and his son Henry, the first Duke of that title, in the middle of the 14th century. He would have noted the Newarke or 'Magazine' Gateway, which gave access to the southern part of the town; the 'hospital', or alms house, with its chapel (preserved in Trinity House); and, most magnificent of all, the collegiate church of the Annunciation of St Mary in the Newarke completed only half a century earlier. In Richard's time it contained the tombs of the founders together with those of other members of the Lancastrian royal family and many local worthies, but it failed to survive the Dissolution of the religious establishments

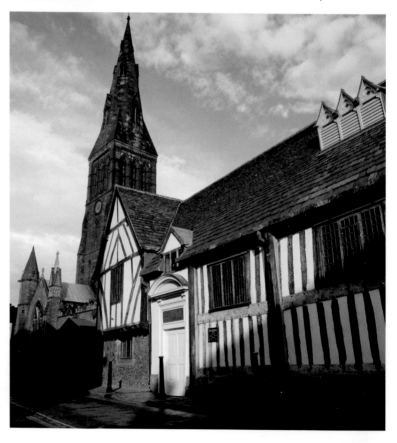

The Guildhall, built around 1390, and Leicester Cathedral behind.

The Battle of Bosworth

On the morning of 22 August 1485, Richard's large royal army and Henry Tudor's smaller rebel force faced each other near the villages of Stoke Golding and Dadlington in south-west Leicestershire. At first Richard seemed to have the advantage, but he was outmanoeuvred by Henry's military commander, his rearguard failed to engage the enemy, and other supporters changed sides. Richard tried to seize the initiative by charging across the battlefield to confront Henry, but was overwhelmed 'fighting manfully in the thickest presse of his enemyes'. He became the last English king to die in battle and the first since 1066.

Before 2010 the exact location of the battle was the subject of much debate; until survey work and extensive historical research (commissioned by Bosworth Battlefield Heritage Centre and funded by the Heritage Lottery Fund) found the largest collection of round shot on a European medieval battlefield. Silver coins, fragments of military and clothing, fittings and horse harness pendants were also unearthed.

This iconic silver-gilt boar badge, worn by one of Richard's high-ranking supporters, was found immediately adjacent to an area of proven medieval marshland, likely to be the marsh mentioned by chroniclers of the battle and later made famous by Shakespeare.

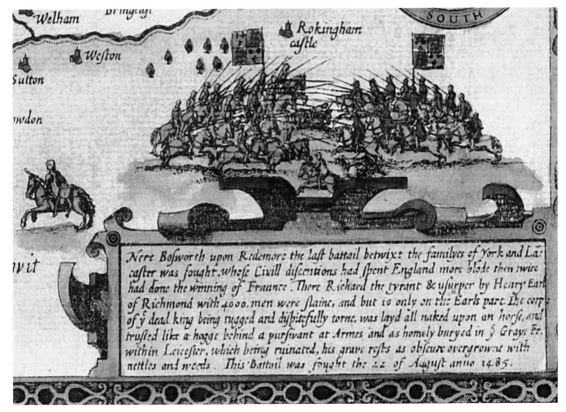

The Battle of Bosworth: a detail from a 1610 engraving by John Speed.

After two days of public humiliation Richard was hurriedly buried in the church of the Franciscan (Grey) friars in a grave that was too small for even his slight frame to lie in. Decomposition may have made haste essential, but it is also possible that those charged with making the cutting simply misjudged the King's height. According to Polydore Vergil, Henry VII's court historian, he was laid to rest 'without any pomp or solemn funeral', but this should not be taken to mean that the friars failed to perform the appropriate religious rites or to pray for his soul.

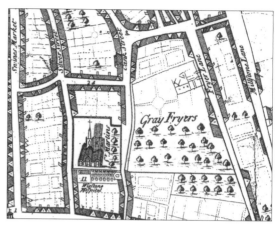

A 1741 map of 'Gray Fryers' by Thomas Roberts. It was here that Richard III was buried following his death on the battlefield at Bosworth.

Ten years later, King Henry paid for a memorial in the form of a box tomb to be erected above the grave of his late rival, but this did not long survive the suppression of the friary in 1538. The place of the King's burial was still remembered when Alderman Robert Herrick, who had bought the site and built a house on part of it, erected a small stone pillar bearing the legend 'Here lies the Body of Richard III, some Time King of England' around 1600 in what was then his garden; but this, too, vanished, perhaps in the battles fought in Leicester at the end of the English Civil War. It was probably after this that the legend that the King's bones had been exhumed and thrown into the river became popular, and later visitors to the town allowed their attention to be diverted to a stone coffin being used as a horse trough, which they were wrongly told had once contained Richard's body. Herrick's house was demolished in 1870 and there was further redevelopment: but the site was not entirely built over and the open space became a Council car park in later years.

T.C. Barfield's 1927 painting shows Richard III outside the White Boar Inn, on his way to battle.

Richard Re-Discovered

In late 2010 Philippa Langley approached Leicester City Council with a proposal that the car park where part of Alderman Herrick's garden and the Franciscan friary had once stood should be investigated. A team of archaeologists led by Richard Buckley undertook an assessment and developed an excavation strategy to explore the site; and the dig, jointly funded by the Council, the University of Leicester and the Richard III Society, commenced on Saturday 25 August 2012. The omens were not promising. A survey using ground-penetrating radar undertaken the previous year had failed to identify recognisable walls, and few thought it would be possible to find the King's body: but remarkably, human bones that would subsequently be identified as Richard's were located on the very first day of the dig.

Skeletal and dental evidence indicated that these were the remains of a man who had died in his 30s (Richard III was nearly 33 when he was killed at Bosworth), and of a markedly slender build. His natural height was five feet eight inches, a little taller than average, but scoliosis (curvature of the spine) would have reduced this by some inches and forced his right shoulder

The skeleton in situ.

Richard III's skull: maxilla wound.

Building on the work of David Baldwin, in 2010 Dr John Ashdown-Hill published compelling evidence that Richard *was* buried in the choir of the Grey Friars and had not been dug up at the Dissolution. Most importantly, he traced Richard's family tree to the Ibsen family, who are descendants of Richard's sister. Publishing their mitochondrial DNA sequence, Dr Ashdown-Hill proved this could help identify remains of Richard III, if they were ever found. His work strengthened Philippa Langley's own research and conviction that the body of the King lay where it did, providing the catalyst for her to finally embark on the project to find Richard's remains.

higher than his left. He was not a hunchback however – the curvature was lateral, or sideways – and there was nothing to substantiate Sir Thomas More's claim that Richard also had a withered arm. The misalignment of his ribcage and the resulting pressure on his internal organs would have caused him some discomfort, but not enough to prevent him from fighting or fulfilling the role of a king.

The victim suffered two blows to the head inflicted by bladed weapons: one was a penetrating wound and the other cut away part of the base of his skull. There were other, lesser wounds to both the head and torso including some, described as 'insult injuries', apparently inflicted after death when the body had been

Open Day at the Richard III dig site in 2012.

> 'The discovery of a king aside, it is the joy of archaeological research, and what we uncover about the past, that spurs me on. It is true that things might never be the same for us again as global attention focuses on our spectacular find, but we are not in the business of finding named individuals. Rather, it is the new light that archaeology shines on how we lived in the past that is also exciting.'
>
> *Richard Buckley*

stripped of armour. Even King Richard's enemies did not deny that he had died fighting bravely; and while the remains *could* have been those of another slightly built person who suffered from scoliosis and who had been buried in the Franciscan friary after experiencing considerable trauma, there was every reason to conclude that they were his.

If the skeleton had been found a generation ago not much more information could have been obtained from it: but today, high-precision radiocarbon dating can pinpoint the age of remains to within 70 years; stable isotope analysis can help establish the individual's lifestyle, environment and diet (by identifying the geological origin of the minerals his teeth had absorbed from food and drink during their formation); and genetic analysis can match his DNA (an abbreviation for 'deoxyribonucleic acid') to another member of his family.

Radiocarbon dating has demonstrated that the individual lived between 1450 and 1540, enjoyed a high-protein diet (and was therefore of high status), and had the same relatively rare mitochondrial DNA sequence as Michael Ibsen, a 17th-generation female-line descendant of Richard's sister Anne. Investigations are continuing, and it is hoped that further DNA analysis will allow scientists to type the Y chromosome and determine if he is related to other known male-line descendents of Edward III.

> 'After a three-year struggle to get to the car park, finding Richard III in the exact place I said he would be marked the end of a long and difficult journey. I am delighted that the people of Leicester will see lasting benefit from the City Council's farsighted support of my quest and I'm eternally grateful to Ricardians around the world who saved the dig from cancellation. The discovery has ignited a whole new search to uncover the real Richard III, the man behind the myth.'
>
> *Philippa Langley, screenwriter and Secretary of the Scottish branch of the Richard III Society*

Richard III: Leicester's Search for a King

A temporary exhibition showcasing the discovery opened in February 2013 in the city's Guildhall. Once the meeting place of the Corpus Christi Guild (a small but powerful association of prominent townsmen), by the end of the 15th century it had become Leicester's unofficial town hall. The oldest parts of the present building are the three eastern bays of the great hall, those nearest the cathedral, which date from the mid to late 14th century, and the two westernmost, which belong to the 15th. Members of staff at the University of Leicester have described the search for King Richard in a video presentation, and information panels give insights into his life and reputation, his death and burial, and the problems associated with scoliosis and ancient DNA. Some of the more interesting 'finds' from the Greyfriars dig are complemented by artefacts from the period recovered in other excavations and an illuminated touch screen interactive display. The King's skeleton has not been displayed, but visitors can learn more about this from another interactive, which examines his injuries in detail, and from a model of his skull made by converting a CT scan to 3D.

In its first four months, the exhibition attracted over 80,000 visitors from all over the world. Richard III is part of Leicester's traditions and history, and local interest has been very high.

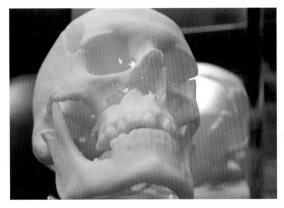

The skull reconstructed by Professor Russell Harris, Loughborough University.

The facial reconstruction by Professor Caroline Wilkinson, the University of Dundee, at the Guildhall.

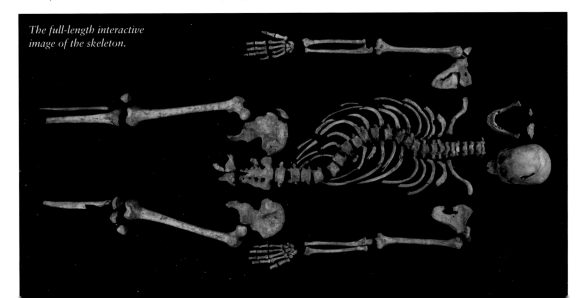

The full-length interactive image of the skeleton.

The New King Richard III Visitor Centre

In November 2012 Leicester City Council purchased the former Alderman Newton's School building, which lies on the site of the Grey Friars church, for the King Richard III Visitor Centre. *Richard III: Dynasty, Death and Discovery* will guide visitors through the extraordinary story of the King's life, his brutal death at Bosworth Field in 1485, and the fascinating story of his rediscovery and links with Leicester. A world-class interactive and immersive exhibition will make the information accessible to people of all ages and backgrounds, and the reconstruction of the King's face by Professor Caroline Wilkinson of the University of Dundee will be displayed after it completes a nationwide tour. It is also intended to construct a small building around the original grave so that visitors may have what one of the designers has called 'a more contemplative and spiritual experience' as well as an enjoyable one.

The entrance to the new Visitor Centre, Richard III: Dynasty, Death and Discovery.

The £4 million project will transform both the inside and outside of the 150-year-old Victorian Gothic building, creating two floors of exhibition space and a new covered area, allowing visitors access to the grave in which Richard's remains were discovered in summer 2012.